Shapes and Patterns

Karina Law

W
FRANKLIN WATTS
LONDON • SYDNEY

Contents

Look out for Tiger on the pages of this book. Sometimes he is hiding.

Everything has a shape.

Bucket

Hair band

Dress

Sandcastle

Spade

Play table

3

Food shapes

Food can be all sorts of shapes.

Squares

Rectangles

Circles

What shapes can you make with a picnic blanket?

Triangles

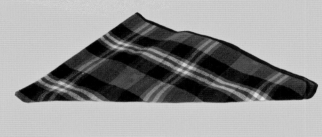

5

Out and about

You can see shapes everywhere.

I took photos of these shapes.

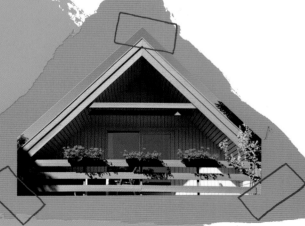

What shapes can you see?

7

Biscuit shapes

Tiger and Rabbit have made some biscuits.

Can you see which cutter they used for each biscuit?

The biscuits
are baked
in an oven.

Now they add icing
shapes to the top.

Line patterns

Some patterns are made up of lines.

A tyre has a zig-zag pattern.

A spider makes a web pattern.

This racket has a criss-cross pattern.

What patterns can you spot in these pictures?

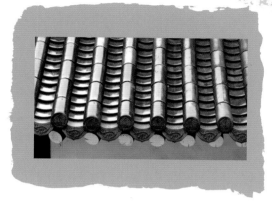

11

Animal patterns

Lots of animals have patterns.

I'm making a stripy tiger mask.

Some patterns help animals to hide.

What patterns can
you see on
these animals?

Moving patterns

Some things make patterns
when they move.

Ed is making flags
with different patterns.

He waves them to
make moving patterns.

Harvey is dancing
with ribbons.

What other ways
can you make
moving patterns?

15

Making patterns

Carlo is using his fingers
to make a swirly pattern.

Jenna walks on sand to make a pattern.

What has made these patterns?

17

Flat and solid

Some shapes
are flat.

Jenna blows up the ball.

Some shapes
are solid.

Jenna has put
up the tent.

Same both sides

These patterns are the same on both sides.

20

Megan and Rianna are making a butterfly print.

Both sides of the print are the same.

Potato prints

Ask an adult to help cut a shape into a potato.

Dip it in some paint.

Print onto some paper.

I have printed patterns using potato shapes.

Make potato print patterns of your own.

Which shape comes next?

Word picture bank

Biscuits – P. 8, 9

Butterfly – P. 21

Potato print – P. 22, 23

Racket – P. 10

Tyre – P. 10

Web – P. 10

First published in 2009 by Franklin Watts
338 Euston Road, London NW1 3BH

Franklin Watts Australia
Level 17/207 Kent Street, Sydney NSW 2000

Copyright © Franklin Watts 2009

Series editor: Adrian Cole
Photographer: Andy Crawford (unless otherwise credited)
Design: Sphere Design Associates
Art director: Jonathan Hair

A CIP catalogue record for this book is available
from the British Library.

ISBN: 978 0 7496 8654 3

Dewey Classification: 516'.15

Acknowledgements:
The Publisher would like to thank Norrie Carr model agency. Jo Stone, Billy, Grace;
Tracy Holyland, Harrison, Harvey; Lisa Walther, Megan and Rianna. 'Tiger' and
'Rabbit' puppets used with kind permission from Ravensden PLC
(www.ravensden.co.uk). Tiger Talk logo drawn by Kevin Hopgood.

Anderm/Shutterstock: 12tl. Paul Banton/Shutterstock: 12tr. Chris102/Shutterstock: 6c1.
Joseph Gareri/Shutterstock: 12c. Jose Gil/Shutterstock: 17br. Daniel Gilbey/
Shutterstock: 20b. Alan Gleichman/Shutterstock: 17bc. Bernd Jürgens/Shutterstock: 6bl.
Stanislav Komogorov/Shutterstock: 11cl. Iurii Konoval/Shutterstock: 17bl. kozvic49/
Shutterstock: 11tr. David Mckee/Shutterstock: 12ct. Sharon Morris/Shutterstock: 13bl.
Four Oaks/Shutterstock: 10c, 24bc. Gina Smith/Shutterstock: 11tl. Mark Stout
Photography/ Shutterstock: 10r, 24bl. EuToch/Shutterstock: 13br. Sibrikov Valery/
Shutterstock: 11br. Joe White/Shutterstock: 20t. Shi Yali/Shutterstock: 6tr. Elena
Zidkova/Shutterstock: 10l, 24br. Ron Zmiri/Shutterstock: 6br. Every attempt has been
made to clear copyright. Should there be any inadvertent omission please apply to
the publisher for rectification

Printed in China

Franklin Watts is a division
of Hachette Children's Books,
an Hachette Livre UK company.

There are 20 Tigers, including me, in this book. Did you find all of us?